The Art Of Authenticity

What People Are Saying

"You are uniquely qualified on this subject, Jason. First time I met you was like seeing an old friend. And every time we talk it's the same. I've always said you are the best (and now, longest running) reality show there is."

- Kevin Rogers - www.CopyChief.com

"Great work dude. You are the real deal online and every time we've hung out, it's been the same. Authenticity runs through your veins."

- Joe Fier - www.JoeFier.com

"Yay! I'm really happy you are sharing this deep truth. Beautiful and full of heart."

- Michelle Edwards - www.yourhumanbeing.com

- "The more I learn about your past, the more impressed I am with the man you are now. Good stuff, Jason."

- Jeannie Martin-Sago

"Beautiful, inspiring, honest."

- Wendi Friesen - www.wendi.com

"Jason, I've always considered you someone who can make people think with their head and their heart and so help people grow in their beliefs. Thanks for that."

- Ryan Lashlee

"Just what I needed to read at this moment in time."

- Alison Sanguy

"Jason is a brilliant writer."

- Peter Platnum Osigbe

"Just the perfect message for me to receive now that I'm back on the road to recovery! Thank-you, this will get me through the hard hours of rehab, I just know it will! Love you Jason."

- Amanda Van Der Gulik

"When I read these posts I get an uncanny feeling we have led similar parallel lives, decades apart. It just resonates. Great job!"

- Thomas Fouts

The Art Of Authenticity Tapping Into The Uniqueness Of You!

Jason Moffatt

The Art Of Authenticity
Tapping Into The Uniqueness Of You

Table Of Contents

Foreword By Kyle Cease

Introduction:

Chapter 1: The Art Of Authenticity

Chapter 2: Why We Lie

Chapter 3: Telling The Truth

Chapter 4: How To Be Authentic

Chapter 5: You're So Money

Chapter 6: Getting Clear On What You Want

Chapter 7: Choosing Your Peer Group

Chapter 8: The Content You Consume

Chapter 9: Freestyle Your Thoughts

Chapter 10: Stillness

Chapter 11: Flexibility

Chapter 12: The Language You Speak

Chapter 13: Pioneering Your Own Path

Chapter 14: Appreciation

Foreword By Kyle Cease

So right now you've decided to read this foreword, and I'm in a studio recording this as an audio.

I really have no idea what I'm going to say right now. But I'm okay with that. If I knew what I was going to say you wouldn't be experiencing my heart talking. You'd be reading something I prepared a while ago.

And I'd only prepare that thing a while ago because I want to say the right thing to you. And the only reason I would want to say something that is right or wrong to you is because I'd want to get something from you.

But if I instead, don't try to get anything and I shift to a place of trying to give, I feel a shift in my body and I allow a space in me to open up, that moves much more like an apple tree.

An apple tree is not invested in how many apples it sells. It's just here to make apples. And that's what I'm here to do. And that's what you're here to do.

And we've been trained by people that our job is to collect and get as many apples as possible, and not give what you're naturally here to give.

And if you ever saw an apple tree that didn't give it's apples, what do you think would happen? It would probably get sick because there's something it was here to do. There's something that the apple tree was put on this planet to do. It's the way that nature works. It's here to actually do something.

And the only reason we stress is because we're not giving our gift. All day we hear that gift inside of ourselves. We hear this voice inside of ourselves that tells us "Why don't you leave this company? Why don't you ask that person out? Why don't you go to a cabin for a while and write a book"?

And that voice is scary because you don't know what's going to happen. Your ego shows up and goes "Well I can't see what that would look like so we're not going to do that."

Because we've been trained that we need to know how everything is going to go versus falling in love with not knowing. When you can fall in love with not knowing and you can listen to that voice inside you, you will be totally free.

Because how boring is life when you totally know how every direction is going to go on a road trip before you go? You won't get to have any spontaneity. You won't get to just move and do different twists and turns and find new people on the way there.

The way a GPS works is it's give you the next turn and the next turn and the next turn, but it won't give you the next turn until you do the first turn it tells you.

There's a voice inside you that goes "Do this one thing".

And you're scared to make that leap. Because your mind can only focus on the loss of that job or that bad relationship or that unsupportive friendship or the city that you currently live in, but it can't see what's going to show up as you let go of those things.

It can't see the new relationships that you can gain as you align with your soul and the new creative ideas you could bring to the world and the infinite possibilities that are waiting on the other side of just that one leap.

If you understood what you were, there'd be a lot of people at the top that would not be able to make a lot of money off of you. Because you would be giving your gift.

And so there's so many people that are here to fight the establishment and I say "No. Don't give them more reasons to keep fighting back."

Instead, tap into your apple tree. Because not only will you not need to buy those things from them, but you will remind those people that are trying to control you that they are apple trees too.

As you access the infinite unconditional love that you are you'll start to recognize in every person the infinite unconditional love that they are and you'll give them permission to access the freedom that every human on this planet deserves to be and experience.

And that's the only way that we will actually be able to shift this planet.

Access your apple tree. Because there's a freedom in that. There's a living in the moment in that. There's a euphoria in that. There is a power in you that's been calling you since day one. And today could actually be the first day that you listen.

Introduction

When I sat down to write this book, I didn't quite know what I was getting myself into. I just started freestyling my thoughts and trusted everything would fall into place. That seemed like the most authentic thing I could do.

The plan was, each day I would wake up and write a chapter. Then I'd publish it on Facebook for the world to see. I publicly announced I'd write a book in 14 days, and invited people to watch along and hold me accountable.

I've never been a great finisher. To get things done I often have to invent clever games or ruses to trick myself into completing them. This book writing experiment is one of them. I'm happy it worked out.

What you're about to read isn't like other books. I considered sending off the manuscript to an editor, but that didn't feel authentic to me. So I left all the chapters in their raw, unedited version.

As you read through the book you may see a couple grammar mistakes along the way. Despite being an extremely well paid writer, I often butcher the English language. I'm getting better and better each day, but I still have a ways to go.

In the spirit of authenticity, I thought it would be best to leave the chapters as is. No edits. What you are seeing are essentially my first drafts. Also, it creates less work for me. Yay! I'm definitely a fan of less work.

Could I make the book better if I spent the time to fine tune it and comb each paragraph for mistakes? Probably. But I feel it would rob some of the authenticity that I'm trying to convey to you.

I don't need things to be perfect. I just want them to be real. And that's what this book is to me.

Also, I don't claim to be an expert on all the things I talk about. Everything I write isn't bonafide facts. Most of the pieces are my interpretation of how I see things. You can take or leave any portion that you resonate with.

I wrote this book for two reasons. The first is to help inspire you to connect with your authentic self. The second is to hold myself accountable on the things I need to continue practicing in my life.

I wish I could say that I follow my own advice all the time. I do not. But by writing and publishing this book it forces me into a position to back up my words and thoughts. It's another one of my clever ruses to help accomplish my goals.

I hope you enjoy the read. It's intentionally short and simple so you can get through it in a evening or two.

And if you love it, please feel free to find me on social media and let me know your biggest takeaway.

Ok, let's do this!

Chapter 1: The Art Of Authenticity

Authenticity, it's a word that's loosely thrown around nowadays. And for many people, it may have many different meanings.

Some believe authenticity is about being genuine and real. Others say it's about being true to yourself.

This Shakespeare quote comes to mind...

"This above all: to thine own self be true,
And it must follow, as the night the day,
Thou canst not then be false to any man."

My version is a bit different. A little less self-centered.

I believe authenticity is not all about you. It's also about the people around you and how you relate to them.

It's how you interact, value, and appreciate them. It's whether you respect, listen and give others a fair shot. It's through flexibility and having an open mind. This allows you to demonstrate your authenticity to others.

In a world full of Fake It Until You Make It's, many seem to be jockeying for position on how to be perceived as authentic. Heck, it could be argued that this book is a play at that same goal.

Your level of authenticity isn't something you determine. It's left up to others. It's kind of like branding in a way.

You can do your best to try and convey an idea or message about a product, but ultimately it's up to the consumer to determine what your brand is. They are the judge, the jury and the executioner when your product is on the line. All you can do is pull the strings and hope you connect with them.

You can spin your PR, write persuasive copy, and do whatever necessary to put yourself in a position to win. But at the end of the day, it's left up to the consumers to decide if you're truly authentic in your sales pitch.

In this book, you're going to discover how to tap into your true authentic self. But I have to warn you, it may not be pretty. In fact, it can get downright gruesome if you're willing to get completely honest with yourself.

This isn't about some clever tricks you can use so others will think you're more authentic. This isn't a promise that people will like you more or buy more of your stuff.

What this is, is an opportunity to get right within yourself. To do your best and serve others in a way that is mutually beneficial to all involved.

Never in my life have I seen a group of people turn their back on a person who's trying to do the right thing. If your intentions are pure and honest, you'll garner respect. You'll attract the right people who are meant to be in your life.

I'm reminded of this story about a priest and a born again murderer. The murderer was released from prison after serving a 25-year sentence for his brutal crimes. During that time, he had turned his life over to Jesus. After leaving the jail, he went to see the priest and was shocked at what he heard.

The priest said… "I admire who you are".

The murderer was dumbfounded!

He thought… Why in the world would someone like this priest, a man of god and good intentions admire me? I'm simply a murderer who didn't value life or others. Surely I'm not worthy of this kind of praise?

The priest then exclaimed that he would never know struggle like the murderer had. He would never know the depths of his lows and how hard it was to climb out the hell he'd been buried in for so many years.

For the priest, his worst sins were having dirty thoughts about women and stealing candy as a young lad. Beyond that, he was straight as an arrow and a goody two shoes. His experience with redemption paled in comparison.

Yet because of the amount of effort it took the murderer to get right with himself and the Lord, the priest had nothing but love for this man. In fact, he even looked up to him knowing what he'd been through. He forgave him the way he knew God would. He saw potential in him.

Whether or not you believe in God is irrelevant. The point is, people will almost always give others a shot if they believe they're trying to rectify the mistakes in their life.

Almost all of us root for the underdog. It's in our blood. It arouses a sense of fairness and justice in what can seem like a very unjust world.

So no matter where you're at in your life right now, know this…

You can change. You can thrive. There are millions of people that will back you up if you're willing to expose your deepest authentic self.

Throughout this book, you may connect with yourself and others in a way you may have never thought about before. It has the potential to free you from any mental shackles you may have placed upon your mind. Or maybe the restraints were placed upon you from societal conditioning, teachers, or religious organizations.

No matter what's holding you back, tapping into your true authentic self is the key to self-liberty.

I'm not here to judge, preach or pretend I have all the answers. I'm as flawed as the next guy. What I am here to do is to poke, prod, and provoke a dialogue that will allow you stop lying to yourself and others.

What is authenticity?

I'm not sure I quite know. I have some ideas but I'm not entirely sure. I'm hoping maybe I'll figure it out while I write this book.

So please don't expect me to be some kind of expert on the topic. I'm simply revealing what's in my heart while I sift through this cluttered mind that often plagues me with too many ideas.

However, I do know this…

People have continually told me that I'm one of the most authentic people they've ever met. Those are their words, not mine. I wouldn't write something like that about myself.

I've received hundreds and hundreds of messages saying the same thing. Over and over again. Clearly I'm onto something.

Whatever it is, I hope to shed more light on the subject as I pour my heart and soul out to you during the remaining chapters.

With much love and appreciation, I thank you for taking this journey with me.

Chapter 2: Why We Lie

I've been telling lies since I could talk. Lies to my parents, teachers, girlfriends, employers, cops, judges, lawyers, probation officers and more. I'm sure there's few people in my life that haven't been caught up in some little fib I've told at some point.

I'd love to think I'm as honest as they come. I truly would. But if I were to believe that, I'd be a victim of something even worse. Lying to myself.

We're all kind of messed up in some way. We all have our own shit to own.

And if you're able to embrace that, you can inherit incredible powers to do something about it. To change it. But without admitting our lies and faults, little can be done to rectify them.

Getting honest with oneself is a journey many people never dare to take. It can be painful and frustrating to truly see yourself. To admit what you've done wrong.

To take a true assessment of where we're at in life, we gotta be honest with ourselves. And that's what I want to encourage you to do today. To get honest with yourself.

The good news is, you can begin right now. Wherever you're at in life. Whatever your status. Whoever you are. You can always get better and better by trying to be a little more honest with yourself.

Despite our backgrounds, you and I aren't all too different in that we seek the same things. We're both seeking pleasure, and trying to avoid pain. Almost everything we do in life is related to these two things.

My self-discovery into my own wicked world of lies began when I was 20 years old. I was dating this cool chick I worked with so I could grow weed in her basement. Our agreement was to split the harvest but little did she know I was about to skip town and leave her with nothing.

You see, I was a bad dude. Since 14 years of age I was selling drugs, stealing cars, and a committing all kinds of heinous crimes. I'd watch movies like Good Fellas or Boyz In The Hood and then try to act them out in real life.

I've had friends shot to death. Watched friends shoot other friends. I even sat 3 feet from my brother as he blew a hole in his foot with a .38 pistol he just stole. The craziest part was that I was tripping on acid while it happened. Then I had to drive him to the hospital and lie to the doctors about where the gun had come from.

Lies, lies, everywhere there's lies. But why are lies so prevalent?

Like I said, we're all seeking pleasure and trying to avoid pain.

So, we lie to avoid embarrassment or punishment. We tend to lie when we seek approval or want to please others. We lie when trying to control a situation that may be out of our hands. We lie to protect people from truths we know will damage them.

There are so many obvious reasons why many of us lie. But the scary part is there's a lot of less obvious reasons why we do it. Subtle reasons buried so deep it's near impossible to tell when we're even lying.

I've always been a grand story teller. While telling those stories, it's easy to embellish a little detail here and there.

After telling the same story for 20 years, the embellishments can grow and grow. Next thing you know, that fish tale you've been telling since you were a kid evolves into an outright lie. A seemingly innocent true story, over time, now becomes a total fabrication.

Why?

For me, I think it's because I wanted people to like me. So, I'd always offer the most colorful version of the story even if I had to exaggerate it a little bit.

Over time, those exaggerations became easy to metamorpihize into full blown fiction. It wasn't until I embarked upon a life-changing journey into meditation that I was even aware I was doing this.

So, I stole all the weed from that co-worker and took off to Idaho to live in a communal meditation group. One of the people in the group was my best friend I had grown up with.

I saw many changes in him after he became part of this group and it intrigued me. I wanted the same kind of changes in my life, but was unsure how to achieve them. This group seemed like my best shot at building a new life.

One of the requirements to be part of the group is you had to do daily meditations. An hour in the morning and an hour at night was required. If we weren't making this commitment to ourselves, we were letting the group down and not doing our part.

One of the exercises I did before meditation was "Watching My Thoughts". For a while, it was hard to even understand what this meant. How do you watch your thoughts?

But after many months and years of practice, I started to understand it. I began to realize that most of the thoughts littering my brain weren't even my own. They were implanted stories and conditioning that I had absorbed like a sponge.

These stories were negative patterns and memories regurgitating themselves in my head. Then they spewed from my lips. I had a lifetime of memories and beliefs just polluting my soul, and then projected upon others.

The process of watching your thoughts sounds so simple. It's far from it. I think the reason it's so difficult is because it's hard to know which thoughts are even our own. And when we have evil thoughts, it's scary to go down that rabbit hole and investigate them. To face them head on might reveal things that you don't like about yourself.

Being an Aries I've always had a high self-esteem. Maybe even borderline narcissistic. I have a strong urge to like who I am and it's always been hard to confront my flaws.

It's much easier to turn a naked eye to some of my twisted thoughts and actions than to reflect upon them.

So how does someone who so desperately wants to like themselves deal with the fact they are a liar?

They have to surrender, recognize the issue and ask for forgiveness. Forgiveness from others and most importantly, forgiveness from themselves. They must make a conscious effort to live a life of truth and find a way to hold themselves accountable.

For me, I'd hold myself accountable by watching my thoughts. If I can recognize the destructive patterns before they make it to my mouth, I have a chance at stopping the lies.

But this exercise almost drove me crazy. It made me brutally aware of just how full of rubbish I was. It alerted me to so many inconsistencies and distortions of who I thought I was.

In a matter of months, I went from this egotistical maniac to a confused kid trying to figure out how to squash the ego. It would take me another 15 years to make peace with it and learn how to peacefully co-exist with the ego. I think I still have another 15 years before I master it. Or who knows, maybe another 15 lifetimes.

Understanding why we lie is crucial if you want to present your most authentic self. Otherwise, you're likely to be lost in the clouds of life and won't even know when your telling little fibs. It's easy to get sucked into trying to impress others or worrying about what others think. When we let these feelings of insecurity guide us, we're on a path to inevitable doom.

Today, I know that I'm still a liar. Even after 20 years of intense work, I continue to have a habitual habit of over-inflating things. I make things more grandiose than they really are. Sometimes it just makes for better story telling. Other times, it's the unconscious mind just doing what it does. It perpetuates bullshit.

Thankfully, I'm honest enough with myself to try and make the corrections when I can spot them. But without continually watching my thoughts, those edits would likely slip right on by.

So if you want to stop lying to yourself and others, I encourage you to watch your thoughts. And ask yourself these questions when a thought arises...

1. Is this my own thought or did it come from someone else?

2. Do I believe this thought?

3. Is this thought even true? How do I know?

4. Is there another thought that serves me better than this particular one?

By examining your thoughts you'll be in a better position to have confidence in yourself. You'll feel more secure with your beliefs and ideas. You'll begin to trust your authentic self instead of over-compensating for the fears within. Like I said, this can be a difficult process. The simple act of watching your thoughts sounds easy. But after 20 years of doing this, I'm still learning more and more every day.

Once you get to a place where you've recognized your lies, it's helpful to make amends to those you lied to in the past. This is where the liberation can start.

The last 20 years of my life seems like one big journey to right all my wrongs. I'm just hoping I can get back to even on the karma scale before I bite the dust.

I remember a few years ago I reached out to that girl I stole the weed from. I searched night and day on social media to find her. It took me forever. When I finally found her, I was blown away! She was about 320 pounds and looked horrible. I barely recognize her anymore. It made me sad.

Her latest Facebook post was a depressing bit about her sister who had been diagnosed with cancer. That made me even sadder. She was running a GoFundMe crowd funding campaign for her sister to help with the medical bills. So I thought the least I could do was contribute to the cause.

I donated $750 which was $650 more than anyone else had chipped in. That made me feel a little bit better about myself.

But what happened next made me feel like an idiot.

I got a message from the woman saying... "Thank you so much for your generous donation. I'm not sure who you are, but your kindness is appreciated by our entire family".

I replied back to her apologizing for stealing the weed operation and being an immature jerk. She deserved her fair share and she never got that.

I mention this donation would in no way make up for my actions. I only hoped that she would see I was sorry and trying to do something right.

Her reply back to me was classic.

"I'm afraid you have the wrong woman".

Hahahahahahahahahahahaha.

I just donated $750 to someone who had no idea who I was. Oops. I guess there's more than one Jenny Owens in the world.

See, I just did it again! I lied.

Her last name wasn't Owens. The truth is, I don't remember what her last name was. But I did really donate $750 to some random Jenny trying to make up for it.

I'm marking that one even on the karma scale.

Chapter 3: Telling The Truth

I'm guessing you've likely heard the phrase "The truth shall set you free" before.

But do you know where it came from?

In John 8:32 of the Bible it reads…

"Then you will know the truth, and the truth will set you free".

Now I'm not trying to give you a biblical lesson here, but that's a damn good saying. There is nothing more liberating than living in truth.

Take my friend Bobby for instance. He's known he's been gay for almost 20 years. But he always struggled to tell his parents or family in fear of the reaction. He believed if his father were to find out, he'd be ostracized from the family.

So Bobby lived most of his life in secret, unwilling to introduce the love of his life to those around him. And this made him miserable. You could always sense a bit of sadness around him, and it continued until he got the nerve to stand up for himself.

It was a snowy Thanksgiving day and the family was huddled around the tv watching the football game. It was in this moment his brother said something that would forever change his life. He said...

"I can't stand this damn Tony Homo".

Now for those of you that don't follow football, this was a jab at the Dallas Cowboys quarterback, Tony Romo. He has a history of choking when the game is on the line, and these type of jokes are pretty typical around men.

But it wasn't just men in this room.

There were little girls present. The aunties and sisters were hard at work preparing the turkey. And grandma was half asleep in the rocking chair with her crossword puzzle in her lap.

A few of the men chuckled at the tasteless joke. But little Suzy did not. She didn't like her uncle picking on her team and the quarterback she adored.

And she especially didn't like the homophobic slur. So she spoke up.

This created quite the firestorm and next thing you know uncle Ted is screaming... "GOD MADE ADAM AND EVE, NOT ADAM AND STEVE".

And it was then that Bobby had enough. He couldn't remain silent any longer. His blood was boiling with rage and he kicked the flat screen Vizio off the tv stand.

As it hit the ground he yelled... "I hate to disappoint y'all, but I'm as gay as a $3 bill." Then he stormed outside to have a smoke.

In one brief moment of courage, Bobby did something he was afraid to do for almost 20 years, tell the truth. He was so petrified of the ramifications that he just sucked it up and carried the burden of his lie. But no longer could he stomach it. It was finally released into the open.

Bobby trembled and shook outside while taking drags from his American Spirit cigarette. He wondered what the reaction from the family would be?

Would they let him return to dinner? Would his brothers beat him up? Would his father disown him?

What happened next is something Bobby never imagined possible.

The guys were more pissed off about the football game than the fact he liked to sleep with dudes. They didn't care. And to be honest, a few of them already knew his deep dark secret anyway. I mean let's face it, he never had a girlfriend and he's 38 years old.

After this day, everything changed for Bobby. He no longer had to hide who he was. He didn't have to live under a shell in fear of what others would say or do to him.

He was finally free!

There are millions of stories like Bobby's all around us. So many people are afraid or ashamed to speak the truth in fear of what negative things might happen. But what they fail to see is all the wonderful and positive things that can happen too.

When we can speak the truth, the whole truth, and nothing but the truth, worry tends to vanish. You don't have to cover things up. You don't have to be paranoid about people finding out. And you don't have to be bothered with whether people agree or not. Unless of course you choose to let it bother you.

The fact of the matter is, not everyone can tell the truth, and not everyone can handle the truth.

Remember the scene in "A Few Good Men" when Jack Nicholson screamed... "You can't handle the truth"?

It was a heavy scene. It went like this...

"You can't handle the truth! Son, we live in a world that has walls. And those walls have to be guarded by men with guns. Who's gonna do it? You? You, Lt. Weinberg?

I have a greater responsibility than you can possibly fathom. You weep for Santiago and you curse the Marines. You have that luxury. You have the luxury of not knowing what I know: that Santiago's death, while tragic, probably saved lives. And my existence, while grotesque and incomprehensible to you, saves lives...You don't want the truth.

Because deep down, in places you don't talk about at parties, you want me on that wall. You need me on that wall. We use words like honor, code, loyalty...we use these words as the backbone to a life spent defending something. You use 'em as a punchline.

I have neither the time nor the inclination to explain myself to a man who rises and sleeps under the blanket of the very freedom I provide, then questions the manner in which I provide it!

I'd rather you just said thank you and went on your way. Otherwise, I suggest you pick up a weapon and stand a post. Either way, I don't give a damn what you think you're entitled to!"

Intense scene huh?

While we can't always like or agree with people who tell the truth, we'll almost always respect them for it. Even if that truth is damaging or hurtful.

I remember when I applied for a job as a private detective in the state of Oregon. I thought there was no way in hell they'd give me a license on account of my past criminal history.

The application process was not easy. It required a lengthy test, an intense background check, and references galore. I couldn't imagine a scenario where they'd put their trust in me.

I decided my best shot at getting approved was to be so honest that I'd risk disqualifying myself. But there was a sliver of a chance that my utter transparency would also work.

I explained how my criminal past gave me insight into how other criminals would think. I also mentioned that this was an opportunity for me to give back to the same community I had stolen so much from.

The job I was applying for was to investigate insurance scammers. This was something I was all too familiar with. My experience in this particular niche was far and above what any other applicant would have.

So I blatantly admitted all my faults. I talked about how horrible of a young man I used to be. And I pleaded to be given a chance to redeem myself if they'd just give me that provisional license.

Not only did I bare my heart and soul into that application, but I also employed another smart move. I got references from cops and investigators who knew my story. I had a psychologist I'd worked with for years stand up for me. He knew my deepest and darkest demons and was willing to support me. I sought out credible people who would testify to my character and growth over the years.

And I'm happy to say, it worked!

Once I got the job, it was a bit weird. I realized that the scammers weren't the only liars. The insurance companies were freaking liars too. They'd do just about anything to not pay out a claim if they could.

It was my job to find evidence that people were lying and faking injuries. The problem was, they weren't all hurt. Some people had legitimate claims.

When I began the job, I was all excited to bust the liars. A boost of adrenaline would shoot through my veins as I chased and filmed them across town. But quickly I realized my job shouldn't be about trying to bust anyone. It should be about arriving at the truth. If someone was genuinely hurt, they deserved to be compensated.

When I made this revelation it made my job so much easier. Sure, I was still trying to appease my clients by discovering the false claims. But I also wanted to protect the people who were actually hurt. By not having a dog in the fight, I was more effective in deciphering what the truth was.

It was this same attitude and inquiry into the truth that helped me succeed so fast in marketing. When I began, I knew the industry was polluted with liars and charlatans. It's almost impossible for a newbie to tell who's looking out for their best interest. Everyone's trying to make a buck, and many are willing to do just about anything for that mighty dollar.

I began making a huge list of all the marketers I wanted to learn from. It didn't take long for me to start crossing a bunch of names off the list. It was obvious they were hiding something. All the stories were too good to be true.

But then I came across guys like Gary Halbert, Dan Kennedy, John Carlton and Frank Kern. These guys changed my life by the way they communicated with people.

Instead of just dazzling me with their slick writing abilities, they went deeper. They actually explained how they were manipulating language and marketing pitches. They'd pull back the curtain and show how to craft winning campaigns even if it exposed a few ugly truths. This level of honesty is practically unknown in an industry where so many are full of shit.

My level of trust with these guys was so far beyond what I felt from the average marketer telling me I could get rich.

Sure, this amount of honesty will always repel a certain amount of people. Some people are disgusted at the things

Dan Kennedy will say. It's far from politically correct. It's often insensitive. But it's almost always the truth. And that's something I like, regardless of how grim the truth may be.

Recently I sold two of my houses. They both sold to the first person that looked at them. I didn't use a realtor. I didn't landscape the yard or make the houses look pretty. What I did is so counter-intuitive, it almost shocking.

When each of the guys came by to see the house, I didn't sell them on the features or benefits of the house. They pretty much spoke for themselves. Instead, I spent all my time pointing out all the things wrong with the house. I even pointed out things that the inspector missed.

I pointed out every repair that needed to be done. I alerted them of every fee they'd have to pay. I even told them about the tweekers and meth heads that lived in the neighborhood. It was as if I was trying to get them to say no as quick as possible.

But something crazy happened with that level of honesty. They felt relieved. I wasn't some high-pressure real estate agent making them feel uncomfortable. It didn't matter to me whether they bought the house or not because I wasn't desperate. And this put them at ease.

I was just looking out for them and making sure all their questions were answered. And I did it in a way that no one would ever doubt my sincerity.

I introduced them to the adjacent neighbors because they were my friends. I wanted to make sure everyone would get along.

When you value truth this much, it creates a freedom that helps everyone. It lowers resistance and allows for a true dialogue void of bullshit and shenanigans.

The question is, do you really want this level of freedom?

Some can't make the leap because they're too deep in their lies. Being this honest might mean destroying your family or losing your job. Coming clean about that hooker in Mexico 12 years ago probably won't make the wife too happy. Telling your boss you're selling trade secrets to his competitor isn't exactly job security.

But these type of burdens can weigh you down. And the only way to rise above and feel free is to be truthful.

I'm going to leave you today with a beautiful quote. Here goes...

"Three things cannot be long hidden: the sun, the moon, and the truth." - Buddha

Chapter 4: How To Be Authentic?

How does one become authentic?

To even ask the question arouses a stench of inauthenticity in itself. It implies someone lacks something that they already have.

We're all authentic. I have a hard time believing any one person is more authentic than the next. Some just bury it under a veil of insecurity and disbelief. Others know how to tap into and use it a bit better.

It's not so much a question of how to be authentic as it is a question of how to let your true personality come to the surface. It's all about shining like the crazy diamond you are.

Your core nature is already authentic. There is no one like you. You're the epitome of authenticity. Yet somehow, society and marketers have convinced you that you need to be something else. Something more. You need to be slimmer, stronger, have more hair, have larger breasts, etc. etc. etc.

I'm calling bullshit.

One way to get in touch with your authenticity is to let go. To not seek approval from others and to pioneer your own path.

Do you choose what clothes you wear because a certain friend or magazine tells you it's in style? Or do you make your selection based on what feels good to you?

Do you choose the car that fits your needs or do you buy something that will impress your friends and coworkers?

Do you live in a big house because you think your customers will perceive you as successful? Or do you live in a tiny tree house because you find it comforting and like the sounds of birds in the morning?

So many decisions in life are made to appease other people, not ourselves. This is insane to me.

I've always admired Cartman from the South Park cartoon because he always does what he wants. In fact, it's one of his catch phrases... "I do what I want". Type "Cartman and Maury" into Google if you want to see a silly example.

Sure, I'm being a bit facetious here, but there's something to be learned from that selfish prick. He lives life on his terms. That's something far too many people miss out on.

Beyond focusing on yourself to connect with your authenticity, there's another way I recommend. Uplifting others. It can be done as simple as sending people a nice and genuine note.

Here are 3 simple and inspiring messages I just sent via Facebook right now...

To Michael Fishman:

"Hey Michael. I wanted to shoot you a quick message to tell you how much I appreciate the way you teach and communicate with others. Few do it as gracefully as you do. Thank you for setting such a prime example."

To Rachel Maser:

"Hi Rachel. I wanted to reach out and compliment you on the great job you've done with Clean Food Crush. It's nice to see people helping others to live a healthier lifestyle. Keep up the good work."

To Marshall Sylver:

"Hey Marshall. Just wanted to let you know how awesome it's been to watch your family grow over the last few years. It was a pleasure getting to know you and Erica before leaving San Diego. Loving that Facebook allows us to stay in touch and see all the chapters and growth in our lives. Peace buddy."

Those three messages took me about a minute each to write. Not too hard hey?

And how do you think it made the recipients feel? Likely pretty good. Most of us enjoy receiving compliments.

The key to making this effective is that you have the truly mean it. Otherwise, it's nothing but pandering and fake. I perused through my Facebook feed and found the first 3 people that I had real compliments for. Then I send them those brief messages in hopes to brighten their day.

The reason I do this is because it helps me get out of my own selfish ways. I'm not doing it so these people will like me or promote any of my products. They were sincere compliments with zero expectation of reciprocation or even a reply.

This exercise is almost identical to a strategy I teach to men who are shy about approaching women. I call it "Batting Practice". The tactic can be used by anyone, not just dudes trying to pick up girls.

Here's what you do...

Go to any mall and start at one end of the building. Then go inside every single store and start gift shopping for your mom or a family member. The gift part is irrelevant. You don't even need to buy anything. You just need a reason to be in the store.

Inevitably, a salesperson is going to hit you up and ask if you need any help? Since they're paid to talk to you and maybe get commissions, they're usually super nice. This is a simple way to approach and talk to dozens of people without seeming creepy.

Next, your job is to try and find one genuine thing to compliment them about. It's important that the compliment is real and not intended to get anything other than a smile.

You're not trying to get a date. You're not trying to get a phone number. You're not trying to get anything but that one smile that'll make them feel good about themselves.

A couple examples of compliments would be something like this...

1. I love your smile. It reminds me of the way my grandmother used to smile.

2. That bracelet is stunning. Turquoise is my favorite gemstone.

3. You were so nice and patient with that old man. I wish I were that patient.

Remember, the compliment has to be real. If you find yourself fishing for compliments, don't use them. It must be natural. It can take a bit of practice, but after enough repetitions, it'll feel empowering. You'll enjoy doing it, and they'll appreciate being on the receiving end.

After spending a few hours doing this, you can see how much easier it can be to approach a beautiful woman.

As I already mentioned, the idea of asking how to be authentic seems a bit ridiculous. The pursuit of it pretty much negates any level of authenticity.

It's like trying to discover something that already exists. Kind of like Columbus finding North America and calling it "The New World". It was always there, some just didn't know.

Yet, authenticity is something that so many people feel they lack. It can be so elusive to so many. So we need to address ways for them to reconnect with themselves and give them tools to pioneer forward. That's what this book is all about.

While I can't show you how to be something you already are, I can give you clues as how to connect with your ultimate self. As you read the following pages, I hope you'll keep an open mind and an open heart.

And may you let your authenticity shine!

Chapter 5: You're So Money!

One of the beautiful things about being a human being is how utterly unique we each are. There's nobody just like you.

Some of your greatest powers lie in the fact that you are exactly who you are in this moment. Perfect in so many ways. Flawed in others.

Your journey to this point in life has been made up of valuable learning lessons molding you into who you are. No journey is quite like yours. Not even close.

I never quite appreciated my journey and pitfalls along the way. It wasn't until my late 30's that I was able to change perspectives. As you've already read, I've had a colorful and checkered past. Much of it made me question whether I could truly like who I was? I've done things to myself and others that I was not proud of. In fact, I was downright ashamed.

For many years, I lived in fear that my past actions would define me as a man. That was something I loathed. I knew I had to change something. Today, I've learned to appreciate the hiccups along the way. After all, they've helped me to develop a tremendous amount of empathy for others in need of change.

Instead of punishing myself for my mistakes, I've learned to leverage them into assets. I'm actually thankful for all the crazy things that took place in my life. Without them, I don't think I'd have the kind of awareness that I have today.

No matter what bad experiences you've had, you can use them to help others if you can find the silver lining. And remember, most of us love to root for the underdog. So regardless of how deep down the rabbit hole you've been, there's always light at the end of the tunnel.

I love seeing people take horrible situations and turned them into positives ones. It's freaking motivating.

One person who's inspired me lately is my younger brother Steven. 10 years ago, I wasn't sure if my brother would live to see the next day. He was into heavy abuse and lived the kind of life you see in a Netflix drama.

I'm not going to go into many specifics about his problems but I'll tell you a crazy ass story he shared with me once.

One late rainy evening Steven was looking for a place to crash for the night. Being broke, high, and homeless, he didn't have a lot of options. So he settled for sleeping in a cardboard recycling dumpster behind a grocery store. It was dry and semi padded with a bunch of broken down boxes.

Considering the lack of options, it was the best he was going to get. So he nestled into the boxes and passed out. Sometime throughout the night, the recycling truck showed up to empty the dumpster.

Being so out of it, my brother didn't hear the sounds of the truck. It wasn't until the dumpster was raised 10 feet off the ground before he awoke.

Suddenly, he locked eyes with the driver of the truck. The driver was like...

"What The F#@%"?

And then he bounced out of the dumpster like a jack rabbit and got the hell out of Dodge. He's damn lucky the driver spotted him and he didn't go crashing over the cardboard falls into the back. That would have sucked.

Anyhow, today he's over 3 years clean and sober and helps other addicts to straighten out their lives. His triumphs over those miserable experiences allow him to help and lead in an impressive way.

I'm not gonna lie. I would have been happy just to have my brother clean and sober. That in itself was a huge accomplishment. One I thought may never happen.

But beyond just being clean, my brother grew into a man that I deeply respect for a variety of reasons. The personal growth he went through while doing his step work in recovery was undeniable.

For years I listened to him make excuses and false promises that he could never live up to. I held little hope that he was going to change. I'd heard it all. Every excuse in the book.

But one day, I heard something different. And after hearing this one sentence, I knew everything was going to be all right.

He said...

"I just listened to this Wayne Dyer seminar and... "

That was all I needed to hear. In that moment, I knew he was going to be ok. After way too many years, all seemed right with us again.

I named this chapter "You're So Money" because I do believe that you have infinite abilities. Your potential is uncapped. The only thing preventing us from achieving our absolute best are our limiting beliefs.

I wrote this book because I believe in you. I believe in every single person who makes the effort to have a better life today than yesterday. It doesn't matter where you're at as long as you're steadily trying to improve.

I know it can be hard at times for some people to believe they're worthy. Worthy of respect. Worthy of praise. Worthy of success. I didn't feel worthy of any of these things much of my life.

But we're all worthy. Some of us just need a little reminder and a good friend to help us along the way. Feel free to consider me that friend if you'd like.

There's no doubt about it, I wouldn't be writing to you today without the help of some good friends.

To them, I'll always be grateful. For they, just like you, are so money!

Chapter 6: Getting Clear On What You Want

Do you have a bucket list of things you want to do before you die?

I'm not talking about a bucket list in your mind that you just talk about. I'm referring to a tangible list that you could give someone else to read. Do you have one of those laying around?

Of all the people I've heard talk about bucket lists, few can show me an actual hand written list. Yet many of us give all kinds of lip service to this non-visible bucket list that just lives in our heads.

If we want to honor and increase our awareness of authenticity, doesn't it make sense to fulfill all our deepest desires too? Shouldn't we cross off as many things as possible from that bucket list?

Otherwise, we'd end up feeling empty or incomplete. That sure doesn't give the impression of being true to ourselves and others does it?

So let's make sure we each start a real bucket list by the time we finish this book.

Here, I'll start one right now...

I want to...

Build a livable tree house.

Surf until I'm 80.

Shoot pictures of birds, identify them and add them to the collection.

Find that mushroom that makes women orgasm.

Hike Haleakala to Kaupo.

Hunt and skin a deer with bow & arrow.

Catch 2 MahiMahi in a day on a kayak.

Visit all the other Hawaiian islands.

Help Dominic shed his autism symptoms and diagnosis.

Get married on the beach, barefoot.

Have a baby boy. Name him something manly like Titus or Thor.

Play baseball with my boys.

Write 20 books.

Meet Shep Gordon.

Produce a music album & play all the instruments.

Create a retirement space for my parents.

Learn to paint waves.

Own horses.

Create a mobile phone app dumber than iFart & make a million dollars from it.

Sleep in a hammock along the beach.

Grow my own food.

Build a garage to store and work on muscle cars.

Have family visit Hawaii once a year.

Learn to kite surf.

Learn to windsurf.

Learn to speak Spanish.

Don't wear socks for a full year.

I could keep typing for hours, but there's a good head start. I'll add it to the many others I've written over the years.

Far too often people have no clue what they want in their life. They think they know, but most of their goals and aspirations are way too vague. If you want to manifest certain things into your life, you need to get specific about what you want.

Do you want a wife or do you want a Puerto Rican wife who is 5'3" tall, soft skin, brown eyes, curly hair and works part-time as a chiropractor?

Do you want to someday become a home owner? Or do you want to own a Victorian home built in 1935 on 6.3 acres, in the middle of Iowa near The Field Of Dreams?

See the difference?

Even in my bucket list example I wrote, I could have been way more specific. I want to own horses, but what kind? Clydesdales? Belgians? Do I want a male or female horse? White or brown? Will I feed and take care of them every day, or will I hire help?

The more vivid you envision the thing you want, the more likely you are to get it.

You'll put yourself in a better position to win when you know what you want. Otherwise, you'll end up settling for what you get.

One of the things I like to encourage people to remember is that bucket lists don't need to be outrageous. Every activity doesn't have to be as intense as skydiving or climbing Mt. Everest.

Maybe you just want to take the train from Los Angeles to San Diego and check out the coastline. That's a fantastic bucket list item. Maybe you just want to call your mother and tell her "I love you" at least once a week? That's a damn good bucket list item too!

Now let's face a brutal truth. Making the bucket list is just the first step. Most will never do a fraction of the things on that list. It's sad, but true.

So how do we stay real with ourselves and do the things we supposedly desire so much?

I call it an "Accountability Calendar".

Each day I like to write one thing in my Accountability Calendar that I'm proud of accomplishing. Sometimes it may be as simple as logging a surf session or a Yoga class.

Other times it may be writing a blog post or learning a new song on the guitar. On a good day, I may write 6 or 7 things I felt good about doing. On a bad day, I write nothing. And most often, that one bad day turns into about 45 bad days and the calendar starts going blank.

So, I always try to write one good thing, no matter how small it may be. If for some reason I laid on the couch all day watching sports and drinking beer, I'll do 50 push ups before bed. That's worthy to put on the calendar. At the end of the day, you can always redeem yourself with 50 push ups.

The purpose of this calendar is to make sure that you are living a life you can be proud of. And if you honestly fill it out, you'll have no choice but to face your decisions from day to day. When you get on a roll, you wanna stay on that roll. It feels great!

My brain thinks of it like this...

I envision the bucket list on the left side, and the Accountability Calendar is on the right. In any given moment I have the option of picking something from the Bucket List and moving it over to the Accountability Calendar. It's just a matter of me making it happen. It's the ultimate real life Swipe Right!

This is the reason why I like to make bucket lists that have a lot of easy and feasible things. It gives you the opportunity to build a massive list when you write down every cool thing that comes to mind. Then you get to have a blast while checking them off in the Accountability Calendar.

When I look back at my old calendars, it blows me away at how much memorable stuff I've done over the years. It all happened because I prioritized having fun and doing the things on my list. I'd be willing to bet that in an average 3 months I'll do what many Americans couldn't fathom doing in 3 years.

The rat race of life has gotten so many of us sucked in that we barely do the actual things we enjoy anymore. We don't have time to. We're too busy working, parenting, fixing things, trying to catch up, and stuck in what seems an endless cycle.

Then it all gets fixed with a gracious 2-week vacation. Ah finally, reaping the rewards! Let's drink booze on the beach and forget our woes for a while. Ugh :(

You have to demand awesomeness in your life. And it helps if you know what your awesomeness looks like. I'm sure it's going to look a little different than mine, but that's mighty fine. I'm kind of a weird fella.

I remember many years ago when I first started surfing with Frank Kern he taught me an exercise I'll never forget. I've done similar exercises with some self-help gurus as well. I think I even teach a different version of it myself somewhere on the internet too.

The exercise was mapping out your perfect day. This perfect day would represent the average day that you'd experience for the rest of your life.

Think of it this way...

If you were Bill Murray in Groundhog Day, how would you want your life to look, day in and day out?

What specific things would you want to happen each day?

Remember, this is the life you're going to live forever, so keep it realistic.

How would your perfect day look?

Nowadays my perfect day looks like this...

I live in upcountry Maui where it's not too hot and not too wet. It's a perfect climate and only 20 minutes to the beach. I have a wonderful family and an amazing business I run from my home office. I have socially conscious friends who I enjoy being around.

My average daily schedule looks like this...

6:50 Wake Up At Sunrise & Say Hi To Kids

7:00 Light Yoga / Stretching / Meditation

7:20 Dring Green Veggie Juice & Light Snack

7:30 Go Surfing

10:00 Eat Breakfast

10:30 Return Calls, Emails, Etc

11:00 Work on something I like that makes me money.

1:00 Go eat lunch somewhere outside by myself. Relax.

2:00 Do something artsy, creative. Paint, play music.

3:00 Play with the kids

4:00 Check in on work stuff.

5:30 Spend time with kids until bed.

7:00 Meditation

7:30 Go out to dinner with Lyndsy.

8:30 Have a cocktail with friends close enough to the house to walk home.

9:30 Snuggle in bed and watch something we enjoy on tv.

10:30 Pass out!

Not a bad day hey?

Once I mapped out what my perfect day would look like I started adding up how much it would cost to live this kind of lifestyle?

This is when I had a huge shift.

My perfect life was way more attainable than I had ever thought! Heck, you can do all the things on my list and not even make $150,000 a year.

4 Hour Work Week, here I come!

When I look at my true authentic self, it's easy to see.

I'm a surfer dude who likes the sun and new age hippy stuff. I'm into eating clean food and sharing the stoke with people I like.

That's who I am in a nutshell. That's my true authentic self.

So, if you want to tap into your authentic being, you might want to get clear about what your perfect day would look like.

And do everything you can to check more and more items off that Bucket List.

Chapter 7: Choosing Your Peer Group

Have you ever heard the following phrase before?

"You are the average of the five people you spend the most time with".

It's almost become cliche in the self-help world. I first heard motivational speaker Jim Rohn say it. I've also heard dozens of others mention the same or something similar.

Regardless of where the saying originated, I think the idea is pretty solid. Our peer groups will have a huge impact on the type of person we'll become. They'll also help to determine our level of health, wealth and happiness too.

In fact, Harvard University has been running a study for the last 75 years that has some eye-opening results. According to psychiatrist Robert Waldinger, true happiness is rarely determined by wealth or fame. In over 75 years of findings, happiness is mostly determined by your close relationships.

So, doesn't it make sense to align ourselves with people who deepen the connection to our true nature? Shouldn't you surround yourself with those who make you feel good and push you to be better person?

Of course you should!

When you intentionally pick your peer group, magical things often being to happen. The ends results are often much grander than leaving it up to proximity. Seeking out relationships offers more opportunities than passively awaiting what falls into your lap.

Just the other day I made this post in a local Facebook group to expand my circle of friends who surf...

"Looking for a couple of stand up paddle and surf buddies who want to ride often.

About me:

40 years old.

Respectful of the aina.

Mellow in the water.

I like to ride more small kine waves. I like to stay safe and usually bow out once it gets overhead.

I sometimes surf with my 6-year-old autistic boy on my board. He loves it.

Eager to explore and hunt for waves & hard to get to spots.

Willing to drive, carpool, chip in gas, food, etc.

Entrepreneurial & philanthropic-minded.

I live in Kula but eager to surf/sup all over.

Send me a message if you'd like to connect.

Aloha"

That post yielded a few replies from guys and gals that seem like amazing people. They're exactly the kind of folks that I'd like to have in my circle of influence.

Regardless of where I'm living, I'm always seeking to connect with conscious people. It just so happens, Maui is loaded with them! Lucky me.

One of the easiest ways to start crossing items off your Bucket List is to have friends that can help you.

A perfect example is my desire to learn kite boarding. Two weeks ago, I was at the beach swimming with my daughter Kalia when we met another little girl and her father Tim. Tim just happens to be a kite boarding instructor and invited me out for a lesson.

Had I of been shy and non-social, I would have missed an ideal opportunity to meet a new friend. And, I would have blown a perfect chance to fulfill a bucket list item. But now that I know Tim, I'm dialed in.

Not only will I cross that item off the list, I may find myself a whole new hobby.

So how do you meet more people that can help you achieve your life goals and accomplish your Bucket List?

I meet them everywhere. It doesn't matter if it's in traffic, the grocery aisle, or a door to door salesman peddling the streets. I also meet them on websites such as Facebook, Meetup.com, Craigslist Groups, and more.

I'm almost always open to connecting with another person that interests me.

But first, it's important to ask yourself "What do I bring to the table?

It shouldn't be all about what you can get from anyone. Relationships are best when they are mutually beneficial.

Once you're clear on what you have to offer others, it makes it much easier to reach out to strangers. It also makes it a lot simpler when trying to connect with important and influential people.

One of the best ways to be useful to people is to know a lot of other people. The simple act of connecting two people that need each others help can be a huge act of service. And it's a simple way of leaving a fantastic impression. It's also a great way to make good money too.

I've made hundreds of thousands of dollars by simply providing person A with an item that person B had. Sometimes it really is all about who you know.

In fact, I remember when a buddy of mine asked me if I knew anyone who taught people how to make iPhone apps? Coincidentally, I knew the perfect guy. And he just happened to be selling a course teaching others how to do it.

So I made a phone call and put the two guys in touch. Both of them agreed to do a promotion together and because of that one simple phone call, I profited $16,000! Sixteen freaking grand for making one connection and receiving a 10% finders fee! I reckon the total time spent on my part was 25 minutes.

The people in your peer group will either make you, or they'll break you. The last thing in the world you need is to be hanging around anyone that will drag you down.

Another simple way to surround yourself with great company is to get a mentor. Just about every successful person I know has had an important mentor at some point in their life. Even if you have to pay a mentor or a life coach, it can be an invaluable investment in yourself.

Finally, sometimes the best peer group can be the people who know you the best. Your family. Having a strong family dynamic is something I'm so appreciate of. I'm aware that not everyone has such strong family ties. But maybe, just maybe, this is a reminder that you still have a chance to rekindle those connections.

Chapter 8: The Content You Consume

Have you ever binge-watched an entire series on Netflix? Or maybe you've gone into full on hibernation mode and consumed 5 or 6 seasons in a short time?

I remember the first time I did it. I'd just got stung by a stingray while surfing and couldn't walk. Bed ridden and depressed, I didn't know what to do.

So I power watched 5 seasons of Breaking Bad in a single week. I couldn't stop pressing the play button each time an episode ended. Next thing you know, days and weeks had vanished. And apparently, I'm not alone.

Netflix reported that 75 percent of people watching the first season of Breaking Bad did the same thing. And when you factor in the next two seasons, up to 85 percent binge watched every episode in one sitting.

I'm not going to lie, at the end of the week, I felt like I'd been the one doing meth. I was zombie tired, irritable and wanted another fix. Damn you Breaking Bad!

I also felt weirdly connected with Jesse and Walt, the two main characters in the show. Despite knowing these were fictional characters, how in the heck did I feel so connected to them?

Believe it or not, your peer group isn't solely comprised of the real life people whom you see at work or the coffee shop. Your peer group can also consist of the media you're consuming on a regular basis.

If you're a news junkie sitting around watching CNN for 5 hours a day, Anderson Cooper is now part of your peer group. Same with Wolf Blitzer, or whatever newscaster you routinely watch.

Of course they have no idea they're submerged into your life. But there's no mistaking that you're entrenched into theirs.

And this issue is not just with television. It's with the music you listen to. The magazines you read, and all content that you absorb.

In some subtle way, the media you consume becomes a part of you. It influences your thoughts and your behaviors.

Just last week I got done binge watching Sons Of Anarchy on Netflix. Without a shadow of a doubt, that show turned me angry and aggressive. I usually don't watch TV that has violence or graphic imagery. It brings back bad memories and it tends to put me in a bad mood.

But I somehow got sucked into it. Sucked into it the same way I was lured into watching 8 seasons of 24 with Kiefer Sutherland. It was like a bag of Lays potato chips. Once I popped, I somehow couldn't stop.

And when it was all over, I knew something was different about me. Since I've been watching my thoughts for almost 20 years now, I could tell something was going awry inside. I just didn't feel like my happy self.

So I decided to do an experiment. I binge watched Homeland and Blacklist too. Both are dark and violent shows combating terrorists and criminals. Once again, I got sucked in. But what was worse is that I could see myself changing right before my eyes. I was becoming like the people in the show.

As I watched and observed myself and thoughts, I began mimicking and aping qualities of the characters in the show. This was beyond unacceptable to me. I had to quit watching.

For most of the last decade, I've intentionally consumed nothing but positive programming. It's been instrumental in helping to change my life, build better dreams and to pioneer a more positive direction. But it wasn't easy to do. I had to ditch many of the things I grew up loving. For instance, rap music. 90% of my music collection withers away in the dust bin now. I just can't listen to it without it evoking some type of aggressive or pissed off feelings. So I keep it buried. It affects me too much.

When I look back at my childhood I can't help but think of how detrimental rap music was to the kids I grew up with. One year we were all riding our bikes and playing in Little League. The next year, we were all drinking 40's of malt liquor, smoking weed, and trying to take advantage of any girl we could get our hands on.

Of course, much of this is just what boys do when growing up. But how did we go from such normal kids to full on felons in a matter of one or two school years? How in the world did we think it was cool to be a pimp? Why would we feel the need to have a gun at the age of 15? Why did we look up to guys who were inciting hate and violence?

When I analyzed our surroundings it was blatantly obvious where we absorbed this stuff from. It was learned from Ice-T, 2 Live Crew, NWA and other gangster rappers.

We began replicating the things we saw in movies like Menace To Society, Boyz In The Hood and New Jack City. Pretty soon, we were no longer those innocent Little Leaguers on the ball field. We were full blown criminals who got excited by the idea of pulling off heists and taking from others.

Now I'm not saying it's all rap music's fault. But had there of been no aggressive music or movies I have a hard time seeing where any of my friends would have learned those behaviors. Most of us had parents who loved us and would do anything in their power to give us the best. Yet, we turned into a bunch of little shit heads.

Why?

Without a shadow of a doubt, I'm convinced the content we consume becomes part of us. Think of this...

Let's say you watch porn every day. And I'm not talking about some Playboy channel stuff. I'm talking about hard-core videos with foreign toys, rough sex, and multiple partners. And let's assume that your spouse is pretty straight laced. Heck, they don't even like to do it doggy style.

If you were to watch that kind of porn for 6 months, do you think it might affect your relationship at home? Do you think your sex life might suffer if your partner is not willing to do what those porn stars are accustom to doing?

Damn it right it will.

All the content we consume has an affect on us. Most just don't pay attention to it. We're so overwhelmed by thousands of things it's hard to notice one television show that may be causing us problems.

I want you to do an experiment over the next few months. Think of the 5 most miserable people you know. I'm talking the biggest Negative Nelly's you can find.

Then, find out what kind of programming is going into their head. What do they watch on TV, and on the internet? What kind of music do they listen to? Do they watch the news all the time?

Then, think of the 5 most happy people you know and do the same thing. I'm willing to bet you, more times than not, the happy people aren't camped out in front of the TV. And they probably aren't complaining about what Congress is doing every other day.

Instead, they're probably taking educational classes or meeting up with a group of friends. Maybe they're on a weekly softball team or they volunteer at the YMCA?

I'm not saying happy people don't enjoy a Netflix binge on occasion too. I'm sure they do. I'm just saying they're more likely watching Planet Earth instead of rerunning Scarface for the ninth time.

Chapter 9: Freestyling Your Thoughts

In 6th grade, I had a teacher named Mr. Freden. The kids always made fun of him because he told stories about scoring great deals at thrift shops.

He'd always preach about frugality and was proud of himself when he score a pair of corduroys for 50 cents. He was an odd but memorable guy.

For some reason, I can only remember 4 teachers names in my entire life. And I was a pretty good student. I blame all the LSD in high school. Hey, why do you think they call it "High" school?

There was my first-grade teacher Ms. Wyman. I don't remember anything about her but her name. I'm not even sure how or why I remember her. But I do.

Then there was the 7th-grade physical education teacher Mr. Camp. The reason I remember him is because he was a freaking savage. He'd always joke about giving you extra credit if you could make another kid cry or bleed while playing dodgeball. I'm not kidding. It was insane. And us 7th-grade boys LOVED him for it! The nerdy kids we picked on, not so much.

I remember Mr. Walmer too. He was my freshman automotive shop teacher. He was also the coach of the freshman baseball team. Luckily for me, Walmer hung out at the bar where I worked too. It was a Mexican joint called Ponchos. I was the dish boy and I got to know him before ever trying out for the team. On the first day of practice, he yelled "Moffatt, take shortstop". I doubt he even knew the other kids names yet.

And finally, there was Mr. Freden. One of the things I remember in his class was a creative writing exercise. We would write for 5 or 10 minutes and we weren't allowed to put our pencils down. We had to just keep writing, no matter what came to mind. If the mind went blank and you had nothing, you just wrote blah, blah, blah until something came up.

I'm sort of writing this chapter in that fashion. I had no idea what I was going to write about a few minutes ago, but I just let it flow. I'm not sure where the chapter is going either, but we'll see.

Blah, blah, blah.

Just kidding.

The other day I came across an app called "Flow State". Flow State is a writing app that will delete all your words if you don't type anything for 5 seconds. It's nerve racking to think of losing all that hard work, but it's also an effective way to pump out material.

Too often, people over edit themselves and bottle up their brilliance. They fear muttering the wrong thing or looking stupid to others. So they end up saying or doing nothing and their canvas remains blank. Their masterpiece never has a chance to flourish because they were afraid to let go. Or, they weren't congruent with their own message which creates all kinds of insecurities.

Freestyling your thoughts, whether it be on paper, into a microphone, or on camera is a great outlet to have. When you think about it, it's not much different than talking to your buddy on the phone. You don't worry about what you're going to say when chatting with your friend. So why should you worry so much when you're a podcast guest or making a Facebook video?

I remember once seeing a video of Jesse Elder saying...

"If you cannot post a video about authenticity in one take, then you probably shouldn't be doing the video on authenticity".

Jesse is a thought leader that I've always admired. Often when I hear him speak, I feel as if he's speaking directly to what I need to hear in that exact moment. It's incredibly timely. When I heard him say that bit about authenticity, I couldn't help but shout "Amen".

I've always had trust issues with people who have too many edits in their videos. Sometimes a bunch of jump cuts can provide a more entertaining clip, but it can lack in authenticity. Anyone can slice and dice and edit a video to appear brilliant. But to do a 6 minute or 39 consecutive minute video without a single edit, that takes confidence. To nail it on one try, that takes authenticity.

While the one take non-edited video may not seem as flashy, it's way more believable in my opinion. An authentic person who's solid in their message can talk all night until the roosters crow.

But let's face it, not everyone is able to freely express themselves with ease. The inner critic can often be a person's worst enemy. So how does someone overcome that inner voice and build the confidence to speak what's in their heart?

There's many ways but one of my favorites is an exercise called Kylego. Kylego is a method of future pacing your desires and talking about them as if they already happened. One of my best friends Kyle Cease (the guy who did the foreword for this book) teaches this exercise at his "Evolving Out Loud" seminars. It's an incredible thing to watch as participants remove their blocks and limitations.

They're allowed to dream and envision whatever their mind can fancy. Instead of just talking about it, I'll write an example of how to Kylego below.

Starting now...

"Remember that time I wrote the book The Art Of Authenticity? I was blown away when it hit #1 best-seller status in two of the most competitive niches on Amazon. I was even more shocked when one of my favorite authors Dan Millman told me he read and loved it.

It was pretty sweet to see a few Fortune 500 companies buy the book for their employees. That meant a lot to me. And the first time I saw it on the shelf at Barnes & Noble was a great feeling as well.

But the coolest thing by far was when Ellen invited me on her show to talk about the book. She was so nice to fly me out to Los Angeles and put me up in the nicest hotel in the city. They even picked me up in a limo from the airport.

After self-publishing the book I got 3 different offers from large publishers to write 3 more books. Writing The Art Of Authenticity was beyond just a stepping stone leading to a successful deal. It became the foundation for my business."

Do you see what I did there?

I basically just scripted the way I want everything to go in the future. By doing this, I'm planting seeds in my mind and making this dream possible. It also allows my mind to expand being my limits because there are no rules or anyone to tell me I can't achieve this.

This is an excellent way to freestyle your thoughts.

Whether you keep a journal, write a blog, or decide to Kylego yourself, take the handcuffs off your mind. Let it be free. Let the mind roam, wander and explore the world.

Sometimes magical things start to happen when you Kylego for more than 10 minutes. The mind runs out of the obvious things you might dream of. It has to keep searching. And when it gets past the outer layer and starts penetrating deep, all kinds of wonder can arise.

Same thing goes for writing. The first few chapters may be a little stuffy, but once you get into your groove you can't type as fast as the mind will go.

So don't be afraid to freestyle your thoughts. Go deep with them. Trust them to take you to places you may have been afraid to venture to before. It may turn out to be a journey you'll never turn back from.

Chapter 10: Stillness

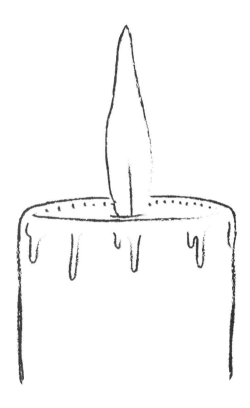

When's the last time you stopped to listen to the sounds of a chirping bird?

When the wind blows, do you pay attention to the breeze as it rustles through the trees and leaves? Or is it just some background noise that goes unnoticed?

If you're like most people, you're preoccupied with uncountable distractions in life. The beauty of the world can often elude us despite being evident right in front of our eyes.

So what can we do to slow down and witness all that is beautiful?

What can we do to block out all the noise and confusion interfering with our authentic selves?

The answer is in stillness and meditation.

Never in my life has there been a day I regretted meditating. Not a single one. But there's been thousands of days where I have regretted not meditating.

It's baffling that something so available, fulfilling and free isn't utilized by more people. I feel like it's almost criminal that more humans don't know about the benefits of meditation. Why we don't teach it in our schools is beyond me.

My first experience with meditation was when I was 15 years old. I worked with an older gentleman named Sylvester from Singapore. We'd wash dishes together and he'd always encourage me to read something new every day of my life.

One day, he turned me onto the author Herman Hesse. It was from Hesse I first read about meditation.

But it wasn't for another 5 years before I submerged myself into the practice. And when I did, my life began to dramatically change.

Over the last 20 years I've practiced meditation off and on. Why I abandoned it at times, I have no clue. It's insanity considering how much I know it helps me.

It's like working out. You know it's good for you, but that doesn't mean you'll always take time to go to the gym. It seems extra lazy considering the meditation gym is right in our minds waiting for us to use it.

Of course, many of us come up with excuses like... "I don't have enough time".

That argument holds almost no weight with me. The reason why is because I think meditation actually gives you more time. Well, at least better quality time.

Too often we go through with our daily routines checked out of life. We're just going through the motions, unconscious of the magic around us. We get sucked into the rat race of life and forget to stop and smell the roses.

Learning to still our minds enables us to appreciate the smaller things in life. And since there's so many small things to be appreciative of, we can always be in awe of the abundance around us.

But if we don't still our minds, we can easily become frustrated and distracted by all the little things too. I've been on both sides of the fence and I tend to prefer the abundant side.

So how does one learn to meditate?

There's a bunch of methods out there. It just takes finding one that works for you. I've tried many, and they've all brought on interesting experiences.

I don't consider myself a professional teacher so I'll avoid even trying to act as an authority. Instead, I'll refer you two places that I think are a great place to get started.

My first recommendation is to pick up the book "Success Through Stillness" by Russell Simmons. You can easily find it online at Amazon.

Russell's story is inspiring and his book helps to make it as simple as possible to get started.

My second recommendation is The Stillness Project ran by a former client of mine, Tom Cronin. Tom's twist on meditation is by far the most enjoyable I've ever taken part in. I just love Tom and the light he brings to others.

Beyond those two referrals, I'll let you find something that you feel works for you. Heck, even if you just lay in the grass and shut your mouth for 20 minutes a day it's better than not resting your mind at all.

I'll admit to you. It took me a few years to even understand what meditation was. I was trying so hard to diminish my ego, but my entire desire to meditate was ego driven in itself. It was often a frustrating hamster wheel of paradox.

It reminds me of a poem I wrote when I was a kid. I don't remember most of it, but I do recall these few lines...

"Meditating be frustrating when you try
Effort alone cripples the whole reason why
Your searching for an emptiness
But found a cluttered mess
Blissfulness occurs
When there's a pause from the mind stir."

And it's in those pauses that we get a glimpse of what authenticity truly is.

Chapter 11: Flexibility

Greek philosopher Heraclitus once said "The only thing that is constant is change".

While this may seem like a wise quote to many, it's often tough for others to accept. Most of us don't like change. We prefer certainty and to remain in control.

The idea of something not going our way usually doesn't settle well. In fact, it can freak some of us out.

Too often we have expectations of how events should occur. We want everything to fit our perfect little plan. And when things don't turn out as expected, we get upset.

But what if we could be ok with things going wrong? What if we accepted the fact that sometimes things go awry?

When you're ok with the unknown and unforeseen surprises, life gets more exciting. And your potential for opportunities dramatically increases.

Us humans are so rigid in our desires and beliefs. Once we perceive something to be a certain way, it's almost impossible to change our minds.

These stubborn ways blind us from seeing all that is possible in life.

It's kind of like labeling yourself a Republican or Democrat. Once a voter identifies with either party they're essentially backing themselves into a corner. A corner that restricts them from exploring all the options and emotions available. They become force-fed the party narrative and most slurp it up like lap dogs, then regurgitate it as gospel. People have lost their damn minds.

Nowadays if a politician is to change their mind, they're labeled a "Flip Flopper". Since when is adjusting your opinion based on new facts a bad thing? Shouldn't we encourage our leaders to challenge their beliefs? Don't you want your representatives to learn and evolve? Or should we just let the same narrow-minded parties argue until they're blue in the face unwilling to budge? Stay the course, no matter what. Ugh.

In life, things change. It's inevitable. And the more you resist that change, the more you'll feed the beast of misery. You see, it's not the change that you hate so much. It's the resistance to the change.

Being stuck in your ways can be it's own kind of prison that robs you of all kinds of freedom. If you want to be happy in life, you gotta learn to let things go. You gotta pick your battles and recognize that you're not Rocky Marciano. Every once in a while, you're going to lose a fight.

This all reminds me of a story.

Most of my life, I hated country music. I mean I just despised it. I'd of rather listened to a lawn mower engine than some twangy country boy singing about his truck.

I thought it was music for simpleton rednecks. Racists. And all things southern. It was not my style at all.

Then one day, in the middle of backwoods Alabama, I fell in love with country music. Heck, I was crying over country songs on the radio.

So what happened?

I was touring around in my diesel pusher RV with my dog Webber, and my camera guy Road Bandit Randy. Randy was following me in his RV with his cat named Bird (RIP Bird, we miss you). He was filming all our crazy shenanigans across the country.

We had just left Fat Tuesday Mardi Gras in New Orleans right after the Saints had won the Super Bowl. It was freaking nuts. The entire city was electric and everyone was partying like crazy. So we decided to mellow out and explore the southern part of the United States.

As we drove through Mississippi and Alabama, I got kind of creeped out. The site of rebel flags was super disturbing. Growing up, I never had fond thoughts of Dixieland. In fact, I hated anything about the confederacy unless it was the top of the Dukes Of Hazard car.

Despite my disdain for all things Lynyrd Skynyrdish, I decided to try something new. Instead of complaining about anything I disliked in the south, I only spoke kind words.

It was my goal to only focus on the positive attributes of the south even when I could see so many negative. I only wanted to say nice things and think good thoughts. I didn't care if I stumbled across a KKK rally, I was going to find something positive in that shit hole. Something like... "Wow Grand Wizard, those sure are nice sheets. Is that like 1200 thread count"?

Anyhow, this positive attitude felt good. I was cheery, and so were most of the people I was meeting. That whole southern hospitality rumor was a real thing. The people were downright amazing.

Yes, many of them were simple. But they were honest and nice. They weren't city slickers like me, and I enjoyed it. In fact, they were so welcoming that I started to feel bad about the prejudices I'd carried most of my life. The people in the south were nothing like the stories I'd created in my head. In fact, I was the one being a short-sighted and racist when I labeled so many people the way I did.

A short time later I was driving through a beautiful meadow on my way to Muscle Shoals Alabama to see a friend. While cruising along the country backroad, a Kenny Chesney song came onto the radio.

Now like I said, I used to loathe country music. Especially Chesney. But on this day, something changed. As I was driving I was focusing my appreciation on the simple things in life. So when the song came on the radio, instead of criticizing or instantly changing it, I listened. And I'm so glad I did.

There's this one point in the song where the guitar plays two simple notes. It's nothing more than a couple quick plucks of a string. But there was something magical about those two notes.

In that moment, I realized the beauty of simplicity. I was overwhelmed with a feeling I'd never had before. All the hairs on my arms rose. My head tingled. And my heart was about to beat out of my chest.

Then my eyes became waterfalls gushing tears. Out of nowhere I belted out all kinds of emotions that had been lingering inside. I was so visibly shaken that I had to pull the RV over to the side of the road.

I'm not exactly sure what happened in that moment but I was forever a changed man after that. It felt as if something in my heart had opened. One of my hypothesis is that it was the first time I truly understood and felt empathy on a deep level.

From that day forward, I was hooked on country music, and particularly the pedal steel guitar. There's just something in that sound that soothes my soul.

I could have easily changed the radio station that day and missed the Chesney song. And I would have missed an incredible experience too. One that allowed me to open up and feel in a way I never knew.

That trip to the south taught me a lot about authenticity. It also taught me that when you're flexible and keep an open mind, you invite more happiness into your life.

Chapter 12: The Words You Speak

The words that come out of your mouth have massive power.

In fact, they have so much power they're subtly hypnotizing you as the words pass by your lips.

Here, let me give you an example...

How many times have you heard someone say... "I'm sorry, what was your name again? I'm terrible at remembering names".

You've likely heard that hundreds of times in your life. And it's quite possible you've said it a few times yourself.

When you say "I'm terrible with names" you're reinforcing a belief in your subconscious. Now imagine saying it over and over again for many years. It's no wonder people suck at remembering other's names. They've been sabotaging and hypnotizing themselves to believe a lie the whole time.

I'm not immune to this either. I often make jokes about feeling old. I'll sometimes refer to myself as Mr. Burns on the show The Simpsons. The joke will be something like... "Oh man, these Mr. Burns hips are on fire today".

While it can seem like an innocent wise crack, it's impact can be deep and long lasting. If I were to say the joke once, it might be fine. But the truth is, I've said a similar joke at least 100 times in my life.

And by doing so, I'm anchoring the belief that I'm getting old into my brain. If my mind believes I'm old, my body is going to feel old. This is something I'm desperate to change. The real truth is, I'm 40 and feel better than I've ever felt in my life. That's the mantra that needs repeating.

Only by watching my thoughts am I even aware that this going on. But if I were to slack on watching my thoughts, it would be easy to slip into this negative pattern again.

Another trap I find people falling into online is their need to rant all the time. I like a good rant as much as the next guy, but if all I ever hear from someone is negativity, I gotta hit the unfriend button.

On the flip side, if all I ever see a person post is positive quotes and success memes, I wonder if they're being real? Or are they just posturing? Even the most successful people I know have a bad day every now and then.

There are a lot of people who teach that you should never display weakness or air problems to your following. I'm not sure I completely agree with that.

I believe there is a balanced rant vs rave ratio that you should consider implementing. Personally, I like to stay as positive as possible. I reckon 70% of my stuff is super positive. 20% is jokes. And 10% are rants or issues that I'm a bit agitated with.

I feel comfortable with this ratio because it allows me to spend most of my time where I'm happy. But it also gives me the outlet to release any pent up anger I may have or work through problems.

But there's a huge pitfall that I witness people sink into when going on rants. And it's even worse when sharing tear-jerking stories about their issues.

The problem is people are inviting others into their troubles but not showing them a way out. If you want to be some sort of thought leader in this world, you need to pay attention to this.

If you're a coach, teacher or mentor you have a responsibility to your audience to guide them to a better place. Not lead them down a rabbit hole of your own misery. When you continually complain and share your problems that doesn't help many people.

What helps others is conquering those issues right before their eyes. I'm not saying you shouldn't share the lows in your life because there are times it may serve you. I think the painful experiences can be a great galvanizer that connects people together. But it's imperative that you're not just inviting people to be a spectator of your problems. Otherwise, you're just going to add to theirs.

You want to bring the spectators along for the entire hero's journey. People will empathize with your struggle if they believe you can rise above it. Otherwise, you're going to sound like a whiner and few want to root on the loser.

I've often had people say to me...

"Wow, you're so authentic and willing to share the deepest and darkest secrets in your life. How do you do that"?

The thing they don't realize is, it's not about the dark secrets. It's much more about the liberating feeling of letting them go. I reveal the difficult stories to lighten the burden I feel of carrying them around.

Once I air out all my dirty laundry, it doesn't feel so overwhelming. Now I can put together a plan to clean it up and fold it away. And hopefully, someone learns a lesson along the way.

There are a couple other points I want to make about the importance of the words we use.

The other day I walked into the grocery store and asked the heavy set clerk.... "How's your day"?

He replied... "I'm okay".

He wasn't fine, fantastic or jumping for joy. He was just okay. And who knows, maybe he was having a bad day. But I'm willing to bet that's his go-to default answer.

What if instead of saying "I'm okay" he said... "Thank you for asking. I'm having a splendid day and I'm guessing it's only going to get better"!

Not only would that answer put me in better spirits, it would set himself up to have an epic rest of the day.

What if he responded like that all the time? Can you imagine how much different his outlook might be like if he just adjusted a few words?

Another example that I saw the other day was a guy saying...

"Aw man, I have to go to work today".

I can understand not wanting to go to work. I fully get it. But complaining about it makes it so much worse.

What if instead he said... "I get to go to work today".

See the difference? See the appreciation displayed by simply changing the word "have" to "get"?

It works with almost anything. Try it.

I have to take a shower. Or, I get to take a shower.

I have to babysit the kids. Or, I get to babysit the kids.

I have to paint the house. Or, I get to paint the house.

By being conscious of the words you use, you can speak in a way that empowers you instead of crippling you.

Another thing we should talk about is the word "I". It's used way too much. And I'm just as guilty as the rest. See,

I just did it again. And again. In a me me me world, it's difficult to communicate without the word I.

But you should try.

Find a piece of writing you've done and take a look at all the times you said "I". Then, see if there's any way to replace it with "you" or something else.

Does the writing now feel less egotistical?

Doing this can be an eye-opening experience into how much we focus on ourselves. Most of the time, your writing should focus on reader, not you.

Notice that I said most of the time. Another big mistake I see people make is talking definitively too often. There are times when being definitive is a great asset. Especially when you're talking about technical info, or trying to reassure someone's confidence.

But there are also times when it makes you sound like a presumptuous asshole.

Look at these two statements...

Democrats want everything given to them for free.

And…

Republicans are greedy.

Broad strokes huh?

Lots of times you can clean up these definitive statements by just adjusting a word or two. For example, in one of the paragraphs above I wrote...

"Doing this can be an eye-opening experience."

Originally it read...

"Doing this is an eye-opening experience"

I deleted the word "is" and replaced it with "can be". Do you see the difference it makes? For most people it will be eye opening. For others, it won't make a difference.

By saying "is" instead of "can be" I'm locking myself into that statement. There's no flexibility there. So it's helpful to be careful anytime you make a definitive statement.

Remember, your words can have extreme power on you and others. The things you say can either lift people up or they can drag them down. You get to choose.

Chapter 13: Pioneering Your Own Path

The worst thing you can do as a hip hop artists is to bite another emcee's rhymes. It's just not tolerated. If someone attempts to do it, they get squashed.

Same thing goes for comedians. Carlos Mencia's whole career began to plummet into the shitter the moment Joe Rogan called him a thief on YouTube. He was forever known as Carlos Menstealia after that.

Growing up as a rapper and a comedian, I always did my best to be unique. Heck, my ego was so big I always thought I was better than the competition anyway. Why in the heck would I want to copy some inferior material?

When I got into the marketing world I was flabbergasted by what I saw. Copying seemed to be not only tolerated, but was encouraged by copywriters. They call it swiping. Most professional writers call it plagiarism.

The logic behind swiping is that you want to model what is already successful. But when you model something too closely, you ruin a piece of your own authenticity in the process. You become like everyone else.

It's easy to see why it's done though. There's lots of money up for grabs. And when you see someone collect a huge piece of that pie, it's difficult to not want to replicate the success.

I'll admit it, I've swiped a bunch of things in the marketing world. I reckon it's because of two reasons.

Greed and laziness.

I've made a lot of money by borrowing bits and pieces from world renown copywriters. I never stole an entire promo, but a headline here or a guarantee there was somehow justified.

To be honest, it never made me feel good. No matter how many thousands of dollars I made, it still irks me a bit. I always wanted to be the guy writing the works that others would steal from. Not the other way around.

Inevitably, I dropped my pride and opted for the fat bulge in the wallet. While it may have made for some quick cash injections, I'm not sure it was all that helpful in the bigger picture.

Because of swiping, I believe my skills diminished quite a bit. I became a commodity writer like so many others. Sure, I was still better than most and made good money, but I felt like a fraud. In my mind, I was the emcee who was biting rhymes.

Truth be told, I think I was a way better writer in my early twenties. Some of the things I wrote back then blow my mind. I'm a bit baffled I even wrote some of the stuff.

But once I began writing marketing pieces, my originality got shredded to pieces. I lost touch with my authenticity.

My advice to anyone venturing into the marketing world is to "DO YOU".

I'm not going to tell you some kind of template won't be helpful. It may. I won't lie to you and say you should never borrow a headline or a bullet.

You probably should.

However, I will tell you that your inner voice is stronger than anything you can copy from another. Your authenticity will suffer if you're relying on others more than yourself.

While there is wisdom in following in the footsteps of great achievers, you should be careful. Most of us don't want to be followers. But it's hard for us all the be leaders unless we've been in the trenches and have proved ourselves.

Don't be afraid of hard work and practice. Every ounce of effort you put into growing is a deposit into the bank of you. And there's no riches that taste as sweet as the ones you made on your own merits.

Chapter 14: Appreciation

It's easy to appreciate all the great things in your life.
Anyone can do that.

But can you also appreciate the not so great things that
happen to you? Can you find the silver linings in any
situation and parlay those experiences into wins?

Every one of us has struggles in life. Yours may be
different than mine, but we all have them. What often
separates happy people from the unhappy is the ability to
appreciate all things great and small.

Let me give you a few examples of what I'm talking about.

About 30 minutes ago I just got done stand up paddle
surfing in Kihei. The waves were kind of small and I
couldn't build up the momentum needed to catch many of
them. They kept passing me by.

Then I saw a big set coming from out the back. I dug my
paddle into the water and put my arms into high gear.
Paddle, paddle, paddle. Dig, dig, dig. Then right before
the wave got to me, I pivoted my board to get into
position for the wave. Then I ignited the afterburners in
my biceps. Paddle, paddle, paddle. Dig, dig, dig.

Then I missed the wave! Are you f#%@!^@ serious?
At first, I was pissed off. Well, for about 10 seconds that is.
But then I realized something...

I exert the most amount of energy on waves that I'm
chasing down and miss. Once the wave rolls by, I'm
exhausted and gasping for air. My arms are on fire. It's in
these moments I'm getting intense exercise and preparing
for even better waves.

Had I not paddled and tried to chase down these smaller
waves, I'd be way less fit. I'd also have a much smaller
wave count because many times I do catch the itty bitty
ones.

Instead of being bummed about missing the wave, I
became appreciative of being better prepared for the next
one.

A similar experience was my frustrations with using
Wordpress to build my website. It felt like a nightmare at
first. I kept messing everything up. One wrong click and
I'd destroy hours of work. I can't tell you how many times
I punched my desk trying to learn it.

But as I look back now, I'm so appreciative of that
struggle. Now I can build my own websites without

needing help from others. I can also troubleshoot other people's sites that may be having issues. And I don't have to pay a bunch of money for custom designers because I can do most of it myself.

When you sit down and think about it, appreciation is so much more powerful than frustration. When you're frustrated, it's hard to learn. It's hard to be open minded. It's hard to do anything well when you're in that state of mind.

Have you ever built IKEA furniture? Did you get frustrated? I know I sure did. But what if instead of getting frustrated we focused on how appreciative we were that we were able to buy a new bed. Do you think that would make building the bed any easier? I sure do.

Another example of counter-intuitive appreciation is all my failed relationships with women. Sure, it would be easy for me to say "She was a crazy" or "She was too jealous" and put all the blame on the exes.

But there's so much more power in accepting personal responsibility. And once I did that, I was able to appreciate those relationships. In fact, I don't even consider them failures or mistakes. They were big wins even if our partnerships didn't last. They taught me how I want to show up as a mature man for my wonderful Lyndsy. I'm not sure we'd have such a great relationship and family today if it wasn't for those experiences. For that, I'm beyond appreciative.

And last, but not least I'm appreciative of the fact I'm a father to an autistic boy. Nothing in life has taught me as much as being a step-father to Dominic has.

I've learned all kinds of patience that I never knew existed. I've experienced an unconditional love that was oblivious to me before. And I've recognized that I'm not nearly as selfish as I believed I was.

The ability to reframe our frustrations into appreciation is a simple thing to do. But for some reason, it feels like a superhero power to some of us.

I encourage you to think of all the things that you dislike about your life and ask yourself...

"Is there a lesson in these woes that could benefit me? Can I be appreciative of this moment and what I can gain from it?"

If your answer is yes, I congratulate you. Your appreciation is a sign of honoring your true authentic self.

And that my friend, is why I wrote this book for you and I.

Aloha

Your Free Gift:

I'm stoked that you took the time to check out my book.

As a way of saying thank you, and to share more, I set up this page for you…

www.jasonmoffatt.com/freegift/

When you're near a computer or if you have your phone in hand right now, head to that page and collect your free gift.

After you open your free gift you'll discover all kinds of cool gadget and toys that I have in store for you.

About the Author:

Jason Moffatt is a internet marketing coach, copywriter, ex private eye, stand up comedian, father of 2 including an autistic child, surfer, snowboarder, magician, amateur mycologist, health and yoga enthusiast, dog lover, and so much more.

He's basically a Jack Of 5000 trades.

Jason has taken his childhood experiences of street hustling and criminal mischief and transformed himself into a change agent for good.

He dedicates himself to growth each day knowing that this moment can always be a bit better than the last.

Hi I'm Mitch, I really enjoyed designing **the cover art** for this book and the sketches that symbolize each chapter.

When Jason asked me to design the artwork for his latest book, I was stoked! He told me the overall concept and layout he was looking for and said that he was orgininally going to use clip art as a symbol for each chapter title; then realized **original sketches** would be much more *authentic*. So, he asked me to create **fourteen original sketches**; one for each chapter.

Having the opportunity to collaborate with Jason was exquisite. I'm horored to be able to express my authentic creativity by being part of this powerfully inspiring book that will live on for generations.

I'm an artist of authenticity and a believer of tapping into who You truly are; designing your own lifestyle is one of the best ways to live the life you love.

I'm passionate about turning feel good ideas into euphoric products; inspiring people to live happy. I create my own products as well as graphic elements for leaders, brands & businesses who share my vision.

I've put together a page for you to learn more about me and the chance to connect with me: MitchMahoney.com/about

Cheers to being true to who You are,

Mitch Mahoney

Connect With Jason Online:

Personal Blog:
www.JasonMoffatt.com

Business Blog:
www.ProfitMoffatt.com

Facebook: Personal"
Facebook.com/jasonemoffatt

Facebook: Business:
Facebook.com/jasonmoffatt

Twitter:
@jasonmoffatt

Instagram:
@jasonmoffatt

Snapchat:
@profitmoffatt

Printed in Great Britain
by Amazon